What Can We Know about God?

Crucial Questions booklets provide a quick introduction to definitive Christian truths. This expanding collection includes titles such as:

Who Is Jesus?

Can I Trust the Bible?

Does Prayer Change Things?

Can I Know God's Will?

How Should I Live in This World?

What Does It Mean to Be Born Again?

Can I Be Sure I'm Saved?

What Is Faith?

What Can I Do with My Guilt?

What Is the Trinity?

TO BROWSE THE REST OF THE SERIES,
PLEASE VISIT: **REFORMATIONTRUST.COM/CQ**

CQ

What Can We Know about God?

R.C. SPROUL

ℝ *Reformation Trust*   A DIVISION OF LIGONIER MINISTRIES, ORLANDO, FL

What Can We Know about God?
© 2017 by R.C. Sproul

Published by Reformation Trust Publishing
a division of Ligonier Ministries
421 Ligonier Court, Sanford, FL 32771
Ligonier.org   ReformationTrust.com

Printed in China
RR Donnelley
0000919
First edition, fourth printing

ISBN 978-1-64289-062-4 (Paperback)
ISBN 978-1-64289-090-7 (ePub)
ISBN 978-1-64289-118-8 (Kindle)

Cover design: Ligonier Creative
Interior typeset: Katherine Lloyd, The DESK

Scripture quotations are from the ESV® Bible (The Holy Bible, English
Standard Version®), copyright © 2001 by Crossway, a publishing ministry of
Good News Publishers. Used by permission. All rights reserved.

Excerpted from *Everyone's a Theologian: An Introduction to Systematic
Theology* (2014) by R.C. Sproul.

Library of Congress Cataloging-in-Publication Data

Names: Sproul, R.C. (Robert Charles), 1939-2017 author.
Title: What can we know about God? / by R.C. Sproul.
Description: First edition. | Orlando, FL : Reformation Trust Publishing,
2017. | Series: Crucial questions ; No. 27 | Includes bibliographical references.
Identifiers: LCCN 2017023439 | ISBN 9781567698381
Subjects: LCSH: God (Christianity)
Classification: LCC BT103 .S695 2017 | DDC 231--dc23
LC record available at https://lccn.loc.gov/2017023439

Contents

Chapter One

Knowledge
of God

Several years ago, a well-known Christian school invited me to address the faculty and administration on this question: "What is a Christian college or university?" Upon my arrival, the dean gave me a tour of the campus. During the tour, I noticed this inscription on a set of office doors: "Department of Religion." When it came time to address the faculty that evening, I mentioned the inscription I had seen, and I asked whether the department had always been called by that name. An older faculty member replied that years ago the department had been called the "Department of Theology." No one could tell me why the department name had been changed.

"Religion" or "theology"—what difference does it make? In the academic world, the study of religion has traditionally come under the broader context of either sociology or anthropology, because religion has to do with the worship practices of human beings in particular environments. Theology, by contrast, is the study of God. There is a big difference between studying human apprehensions of religion and studying the nature and character of God Himself. The first is purely natural in its orientation. The second is supernatural, dealing with what lies above and beyond the things of this world.

After explaining this in my lecture to the faculty, I added that a true Christian college or university is committed to the premise that the ultimate truth is the truth of God, and that He is the foundation and source of all other truth. Everything we learn—economics, philosophy, biology, mathematics—has to be understood in light of the overarching reality of the character of God. That is why, in the Middle Ages, theology was called "the queen of the sciences" and philosophy "her handmaiden." Today the queen has been deposed from her throne and, in many cases, driven into exile, and a supplanter now reigns. We have replaced theology with religion.

Theology Defined

The word *theology* shares a suffix, *-ology*, with the names of many disciplines and sciences, such as *biology*, *physiology*, and *anthropology*. The suffix comes from the Greek word *logos*, which we find in the opening of John's gospel: "In the beginning was the Word, and the Word was with God, and the Word was God" (John 1:1). The Greek word *logos* means "word" or "idea," or, as one philosopher translated it, "logic" (it is also the term from which we get the English word *logic*). So when we study biology, we are looking at the word or the logic of life. Anthropology is the word or logic about humans, *anthrōpos* being the Greek word for *man*. The primary part of the word *theology* comes from the Greek *theos*, which means "god," so theology is the study of the word or logic of God Himself.

Theology is a very broad term. It refers not only to God but to all God has revealed to us in sacred Scripture. Included in the discipline of theology is the study of Christ, which we call "Christology." It also includes the study of the Holy Spirit, which we call "pneumatology," the study of sin, which is called "hamartiology," and the study of future things, which we call "eschatology." Those are subdivisions of theology. In this booklet, we are concerned with "theology proper," which has specific reference to the study of God Himself.

The content that theologians study in order to do theology is God's revelation. God has plainly revealed His existence to every creature on earth; all people know that He exists, whether or not they acknowledge it. However, we need to move beyond the knowledge that God exists and come to a deeper understanding of who He is—His character and nature—because no aspect of theology defines everything else as comprehensively as our understanding of God. In fact, only as we understand the character of God can we understand every other doctrine properly.

God Incomprehensible

Historically, the first undertaking for theologians is the study of the incomprehensibility of God. At first glance, such an undertaking appears contradictory; how can one study something that is incomprehensible? However, this pursuit makes sense when we grasp that theologians use the term *incomprehensible* in a narrower and more precise way than it is used in everyday speech. Theologically speaking, *incomprehensible* does not mean that we cannot know anything about God but rather that our knowledge of Him will always be limited. We can have an apprehensive, meaningful knowledge of God, but we can never, not even in heaven, have an exhaustive knowledge of Him; we cannot totally comprehend all that He is.

One reason for that was articulated by John Calvin in the phrase *finitum non capax infinitum*, which means "the finite cannot grasp the infinite." The phrase can be interpreted in two distinct ways because the word *capax* can be translated either as "contain" or as "grasp." An eight-ounce glass cannot possibly contain an infinite amount of water because it has only a finite volume; the finite cannot contain the infinite. But when Calvin's phrase is translated with the other meaning of *capax*, "grasp," it indicates that God cannot be grasped in His totality. Our minds are finite, lacking the capacity to grasp or understand all that God is. His ways are not our ways. His thoughts are not our thoughts. He surpasses our ability to comprehend Him in His fullness.

God Revealed

Since the finite cannot grasp the infinite, how can we, as finite human beings, learn anything about God or have any significant or meaningful knowledge of who He is? Calvin said that God in His graciousness and mercy condescends to lisp for our benefit. In other words, He addresses us on our terms and in our own language, just as a parent might coo when talking to an infant. We call it "baby talk"; nevertheless, something meaningful and intelligible is communicated.

We find this idea in the Bible's anthropomorphic language. *Anthropomorphic* comes from the Greek word *anthrōpos*, which means "man," "mankind," or "human," and *morphology* is the term for the study of forms and shapes. Therefore, we can easily see that anthropomorphic simply means "in human form." When we read in Scripture that the heavens are God's throne and the earth is His footstool (Isa. 66:1), we imagine a massive deity seated in heaven and stretching out His feet on the earth, but we do not really think that is what God is like. Likewise, we read that God owns the cattle on a thousand hills (Ps. 50:10), but we do not interpret that to mean that He is a great cattle rancher who comes down and has a shootout with the devil every now and then. To the contrary, that image communicates to us that God is powerful and self-sufficient just like a human rancher who owns vast herds of cattle.

The Scriptures tell us that God is not a man—He is spirit (John 4:24) and therefore not physical—yet He is often described with physical attributes. There are mentions of His eyes, His head, His strong right arm, His feet, and His mouth. Scripture speaks of God as having not only physical attributes but also emotional attributes. We read in places of God's repenting, yet elsewhere in the Bible we are told that God does not change His mind. God is described in human terms in certain instances in the Bible because it is the only way man knows to speak about God.

We must be careful to understand what the Bible's anthropomorphic language conveys. On the one hand, the Bible affirms what these forms communicate about God. On the other hand, in a more didactic way, it warns us that God is not a man. However, this does not mean that abstract, technical, theological language is superior to anthropomorphic language, so that we are better off saying, "God is omnipotent," rather than "God owns the cattle on a thousand hills." The only way we can understand the word *omni* or *all* is by our human ability to understand what *all* means. Similarly, we do not conceive of power in the same way God conceives of power. He has an infinite understanding of power, whereas we have a finite understanding of it.

For all these reasons, God does not speak to us in His language; He speaks to us in ours. And because He speaks to us in the only language we can understand, we are able to grasp it. In other words, all biblical language is anthropomorphic, and all language about God is anthropomorphic, because the only language we have at our disposal is anthropomorphic language, and that is because we are human beings.

Because of these limits imposed by the gulf between the infinite God and finite human beings, the church has had to be careful in how it seeks to describe God.

One of the most common ways to describe God is called the *via negationis*. A *via* is a "road" or "way." The word *negationis* simply means "negation," which is a primary way we speak about God. In other words, we describe God by saying what He is not. For example, we have noted that God is infinite, which means "not finite." Similarly, human beings change over time. They undergo mutations, so they are called "mutable." God, however, does not change, so

He is immutable, which means "not mutable." Both terms, infinite and immutable, describe God by what He is not.

There are two other ways that systematic theologians speak of God. One is called the *via eminentiae*, "the way of eminence," in which we take known human concepts or references to the ultimate degree, such as the terms omnipotence and omniscience. Here, the word for "power," *potentia*, and the word for "knowledge," *scientia*, are taken to the ultimate degree, *omni*, and applied to God. He is all-powerful and all-knowing, whereas we are only partially powerful and knowing.

The third way is the *via affirmationis*, or "way of affirmation," whereby we make specific statements about the character of God, such as "God is one," "God is holy," and "God is sovereign." We positively attribute certain characteristics to God and affirm that they are true of Him.

Three Forms of Speech

In considering God's incomprehensibility, it is important to note three distinct forms of human speech that the church has delineated: univocal, equivocal, and analogical.

Univocal language refers to the use of a descriptive

term that, when applied to two different things, renders the same meaning. For example, to call a dog "good" and a cat "good" is to say they both are obedient.

Equivocal speech refers to the use of a term that changes radically in its meaning when used for two different things. If you went to hear a dramatic poetry reading but were disappointed with the performance, you might say, "That was a bald narrative." You certainly would not mean that the narrator had no hair on his head; you would mean that something was lacking. There was no pizzazz or passion. Just as something is lacking on the head of a bald person—namely, hair—so there was something lacking in the dramatic reading. You are employing a metaphorical use of the word *bald*, and in so doing you are moving far away from the meaning of the word when it is applied to hair.

In between univocal speech and equivocal speech is analogical speech. An analogy is a representation based on proportion. The meaning changes in direct proportion to the difference of the things being described. A man and a dog may both be good, but their goodness is not exactly the same. When we say that God is good, we mean that His goodness is like or similar to our goodness, not identical but enough like ours that we can talk meaningfully with each other about it.

The fundamental principle is that even though we do not know God exhaustively and comprehensively, we do have meaningful ways of speaking about Him. God has addressed us in our terms, and, because He has made us in His image, there is an analogy that opens for us an avenue of communication with Him.

One in Essence

When we look at the cultures of antiquity, we cannot help but notice a highly developed system of polytheism. We think, for example, of the Greeks, who had their pantheon of deities, and of the Romans, who had their corresponding gods and goddesses covering every sphere of human concern and endeavor. In the midst of that ancient Mediterranean world, one culture—the Jewish culture—stands out for its uniquely developed commitment to monotheism.

Some critical scholars argue that the Jewish religion as

reflected in the Old Testament was not really monotheistic but was a subtle blending of forms of polytheism. These critics claim that the Scriptures as we have them today were worked over by later editors who wrote a more modern view of monotheism back into the patriarchal accounts in the biblical record. Those critical theories notwithstanding, from the first page of Scripture we find an unambiguous declaration that there are no limits on the reign and authority of the Lord God. He is the God of heaven and earth, the One who creates and rules all things.

Unity and Uniqueness

Great emphasis was placed on God's uniqueness in the Old Testament community of Israel. We think, for example, of the *Shema* in the book of Deuteronomy. The *Shema* was recited in Israelite liturgy and was deeply rooted in the consciousness of the people: "Hear, O Israel: The Lord our God, the Lord is one. You shall love the Lord your God with all your heart and with all your soul and with all your might" (Deut. 6:4–5). Those words also constitute the Great Commandment (Matt. 22:37). After declaring the *Shema*, Moses adds:

And these words that I command you today shall be on your heart. You shall teach them diligently to your children, and shall talk of them when you sit in your house, and when you walk by the way, and when you lie down, and when you rise. You shall bind them as a sign on your hand, and they shall be as frontlets between your eyes. You shall write them on the doorposts of your house and on your gates. (Deut. 6:6–9)

This announcement of the nature of God—His unity and uniqueness—was so central to the religious life of the people that this point was to be given by way of instruction to the children on a daily basis. The people were to put it on their wrists, on their foreheads, and on their doorposts; in other words, they were to think and talk about it all the time. Israelite parents were to make sure that their children understood the uniqueness of God so that this truth would permeate the community in each generation. The polytheism in the false religions of the nations all around them was seductive, as the Old Testament reveals. The greatest threat to Israel was the corruption that came from pursuing false gods. Israel needed to remember there was no God except its God.

The uniqueness of God is also exhibited in the first of the Ten Commandments: "You shall have no other gods before me" (Ex. 20:3). The commandment does not mean that God's people can have other gods so long as Yahweh is ranked first. "Before me" means "in my presence," and the presence of Yahweh extends throughout the entire creation. So when God said, "You shall have no other gods before me," He was saying that there are no other gods because He alone reigns as deity.

The Trinity

The Old Testament stresses monotheism, yet we confess our faith in a triune God. The doctrine of the Trinity, one of the most mysterious doctrines of the Christian faith, has caused no small amount of controversy throughout church history. Some of the controversy stems from misunderstanding the Trinity as three distinct gods—Father, Son, and Holy Spirit. This idea is called "tritheism," which is a form of polytheism.

How can the Christian church affirm the Trinity, that God is Father, Son, and Holy Spirit? The doctrine of the Trinity is established by the New Testament itself. The

New Testament speaks of God in terms of the Father, the Son, and the Holy Spirit. No text expresses this concept more clearly than the opening chapter of John's gospel, the prologue of which sets the stage for the church's confession of faith in the Trinity:

> In the beginning was the Word, and the Word was with God, and the Word was God. He was in the beginning with God. All things were made through him, and without him was not any thing made that was made. In him was life, and the life was the light of men. The light shines in the darkness, and the darkness has not overcome it. (John 1:1–5)

We translate the Greek word *logos* as "word," so the actual Greek reads: "In the beginning was the *logos*, and the *logos* was with God, and the *logos* was God." John makes a distinction between God and the *logos*. The Word and God are together yet distinct—"the Word was *with* God."

The word *with* may seem insignificant, but in the Greek language there are at least three terms that can be translated by the English *with*. There is *sun*, which comes across as the English prefix *syn-*. We find that prefix in *synchronize*, which means "to occur at the same time"; we synchronize our watches to gather at the same time. The Greek word *meta* is also translated as "with." In the term *metaphysics*, *meta* is used in the sense of being alongside of. A third word for "with" used by the Greeks is *pros*, which forms the basis of another Greek word, *prosōpon*, which means "face." This use of *with* connotes a face-to-face relationship, which is the most intimate way in which people can be together. It is this term John uses when he writes, "In the beginning was the Word, and the Word was with God." By using *pros*, John is indicating that the *logos* was in the closest possible relationship to God.

So we see that the *logos* was with God from the beginning in an intimate relationship, but the next clause seems to confuse that: "and the Word [the *logos*] was God." Here John uses a common form of the Greek verb "to be," a linking verb used here in the copulative sense. This means that what is affirmed in the predicate is found in the subject, such that they are reversible: "The Word was God and God was the Word." This is a clear ascription of deity to the Word. The Word is differentiated from God, but the Word is also identified with God.

The church developed the doctrine of the Trinity not

only from this New Testament text but also from many others. Of all the descriptive terms used for Jesus in the New Testament, the one that dominated the thinking of theologians during the first three hundred years of church history was *logos*, because it gives such an exalted view of the nature of Christ.

John also gives us the response of Thomas in the upper room. Thomas was skeptical about the reports he had received from the women and from his friends of the resurrection of Christ, and he said, "Unless I see in his hands the mark of the nails, and place my finger into the mark of the nails, and place my hand into his side, I will never believe" (John 20:25). When Christ appeared and showed His wounded hands to Thomas and invited Thomas to put his hand into His wounded side, Thomas cried out, "My Lord and my God!" (v. 28).

The New Testament writers, particularly the Jewish ones, were acutely conscious not only of the first commandment of the Old Testament but also of the second commandment, the warning against making graven images. The prohibition against all forms of idolatry—creature worship—is deeply rooted in the Old Testament. Because of that, the New Testament writers were aware that Christ can be worshiped only if He is divine, so the fact that Jesus accepted the worship of Thomas is significant.

When Jesus healed on the Sabbath and forgave sin, some of the scribes objected and said, "Who can forgive sins but God alone?" (Mark 2:7). Every Jew understood that the Lord of the Sabbath is God, the One who had instituted the Sabbath, so when Jesus explained that He had healed the man "that you may know that the Son of Man has authority on earth to forgive sins," He was declaring His deity (v. 10). Many reacted in anger because Jesus was claiming authority that belongs only to God.

When John writes, "He was in the beginning with God. All things were made through him, and without him was not any thing made that was made," the *logos* is identified with the Creator. John also says, "In Him was life." To say that life is in the *logos*, that the *logos* is the source of life, is clearly to attribute deity to this One called "the Word."

In a similar fashion, the New Testament attributes deity to the Holy Spirit. This is often done by ascribing to the Spirit attributes that pertain to God alone, including holiness (Matt. 12:32), eternality (Heb. 9:14), omnipotence (Rom. 15:18–19), and omniscience (John 14:26). The divinity of the Holy Spirit is also demonstrated when He is placed on the same level with the Father and Son, as in the baptismal formula in Matthew 28:18–20 or Paul's benediction in 2 Corinthians 13:14.

Chapter Three

Three in Person

Some time ago, a professor of philosophy shared with me his view that the doctrine of the Trinity is a contradiction and that intelligent people do not embrace contradictions. I agreed with him that intelligent people should not embrace contradictions. I was surprised, however, that he classified the doctrine of the Trinity as a contradiction, because, as a philosopher, he had been trained in the discipline of logic and therefore knew the difference between a contradiction and a paradox.

The formula for the Trinity is paradoxical, but it is by no means contradictory. The law of noncontradiction states that something cannot be what it is and not be what it is at the same time and in the same relationship. For instance, I can be a father and a son at the same time, but not in the same relationship. The historic formula is that God is one in essence and three in person; He is one in one way and three in another way. In order to violate the law of noncontradiction, God would have to be one in essence and at the same time three in essence, or one in person and at the same time three in person. Therefore, when we look at the formal categories of rational thought, we see, objectively, that the formula of the Trinity is not contradictory.

The church struggled with this profoundly in the first four centuries in order to be faithful to the clear teaching of Scripture that God is one and also that the Father, the Son, and the Holy Spirit are all divine. Resolving this apparent contradiction was no mean feat. At first glance, it looks as if the Christian community was confessing faith in three gods, which would violate the principle of monotheism that was so deeply entrenched in the Old Testament.

However, as I said above, the concept of the Trinity is paradoxical but not contradictory. The word *paradox* is based on both a Greek prefix and a Greek root. The prefix *para* means "alongside of." When we refer to parachurch ministries, paramedics, or paralegals, we have in mind organizations and people who work alongside of others. In like manner, a parable was something that Jesus gave alongside of His teaching to illustrate a point. The root of the word *paradox* comes from the Greek word *dokeō*, which means "to seem," "to think," or "to appear." So the word *paradox* refers to something that, when placed alongside of something else, appears to be contradictory until closer examination reveals it is not so.

The Christian formula for the Trinity—God is one essence in three persons—may seem to be contradictory because we are accustomed to seeing one being as one person. We cannot conceive of how one being could be contained in three persons and still be only one being. To that extent, the doctrine of the Trinity in this formulation is mysterious; it boggles the mind to think of a being who is absolutely one in His essence yet three in person.

Essence and Person

When my wife and I were living in Holland, we learned that people vacuum their houses with a *stofzuiger*, which literally means "stuff sucker." They could have used a more sophisticated metaphysical term, but the word *stuff* explains much.

What is the stuff that distinguishes a human being from an antelope, an antelope from a grape, or a grape from God? It is the essence of the thing, its *ousios*, a Greek word that means "being" or "substance." The stuff of deity, the essence—the *ousios*—is what God is in Himself. When the church declared that God is one essence, it was saying that God is not partly in one place and partly in another. God is only one being.

Part of the problem we have with explaining how God is one in being but three in person is that this formula was derived from the Latin *persona*, from which we get our word *person*. Its primary function in the Latin language was as a legal term or as a term used in the dramatic arts. It was customary for highly trained actors to play more than one role in a play, and the actors distinguished their characters by speaking through masks, the Latin word for which was *persona*. So when Tertullian first spoke of God as one being, three *personae*, he was saying that God simultaneously exists as three roles or personalities—Father, Son, and Holy Spirit. However, the idea of *person* in that formula does not correspond exactly to our English concept of personality, in which one person means one distinct being.

Subsistence and Existence

In order to make a distinction among the persons of the Trinity, other terms have been used. One is *subsistence*. We are familiar with that term because it is often used to describe those who live beneath standard economic levels. A subsistence in the Godhead is a real difference but not an essential difference in the sense of a difference in being. Each person in the Trinity subsists or exists *under* the presence of deity. Subsistence is a difference within the scope of being, not a separate being or essence. All persons in the Godhead have all the attributes of deity.

Another important term for understanding the distinction among the persons of the Trinity is *existence*. The term *exist* in English is derived etymologically from the Latin *existere*, from *ex* ("out of") and *stere* ("to stand"). From a philosophical standpoint, going back before Plato, the concept of *existence* refers to pure being that depends on nothing for its ability to be. It is eternal. It has the power of being within itself. It is by no means creaturely. Creaturely existence is characterized not by *being* but by *becoming*, because the chief character trait of all creatures is that they change. Whatever you are today, you will be ever so slightly different tomorrow, and today you are different from what you were yesterday.

God does not exist in the way human beings do, because that would make Him a creature, giving Him a dependent and derived existence. We say, rather, that God *is*. God is *being*, not becoming or changing. He is eternally the same, so we say He is one being. Theologians speak of the Trinity not as three *existences* but as three *subsistences*; that is, within the one underived being of God, at a lower dimension, we must distinguish among these subsistences, which the Bible calls Father, Son, and Holy Spirit. There are not three existences or beings but rather three subsistences within that one eternal being.

That we distinguish among the three persons is necessary because the Bible makes the distinction. It is a real distinction but not an essential distinction, and by "not essential" I do not mean unimportant. I mean that although there are real differences within the Godhead, there are not real differences within the essence of the deity Himself. One being, three persons—Father, Son, and Holy Spirit.

Incommunicable
Attributes

When I go to the bank to cash a check, the teller requests some form of identification. I usually open my wallet and show my Florida driver's license. One side of the license lists my eye and hair color and my age. These characteristics define some of my human attributes.

In the study of the doctrine of God, a primary concern is to develop an understanding of His attributes. We seek to look at specific characteristics of God, such as His holiness,

His immutability, and His infinity, to gain a coherent understanding of who He is.

At the outset, we must make a distinction between God's *communicable* attributes and His *incommunicable* attributes. A communicable attribute is one that can be transferred from one person to another. For example, the Centers for Disease Control and Prevention in Atlanta studies contagious diseases. Such diseases are also known as communicable diseases because they are easily transmitted from one person to another. In like manner, God's communicable attributes are those that can be transferred to His creatures.

By contrast, an incommunicable attribute is one that cannot be transferred. God's incommunicable attributes, therefore, cannot be attributes of human beings. Even God cannot communicate certain characteristics of His being to the creatures He has made. Sometimes theologians are asked whether it is possible for God to create another god, and the answer is no. If God were to create another god, the result would be a creature, which, by definition, would lack the necessary attributes that describe God, such as independence, eternality, and immutability.

As we examine the distinction between God's communicable and incommunicable attributes, it is important to note that God is a simple being; in other words, He is not made up of parts. We have distinctive body parts—toes, intestines, lungs, and so forth. God is a simple being in the sense that He is not complex. Theologically speaking, God is His attributes.

God's simplicity also means that His attributes define one another. We say, for example, that God is holy, just, immutable, and omnipotent, but His omnipotence is always a holy omnipotence, a just omnipotence, and an immutable omnipotence. All the character traits that we can identify in God also define His omnipotence. By the same token, God's eternality is an omnipotent eternality, and His holiness is an omnipotent holiness. He is not one part holiness, another part omnipotence, and another part immutability. He is altogether holy, altogether omnipotent, and altogether immutable.

The distinction between God's communicable and incommunicable attributes is important because it helps us come to a clear understanding of the difference between God and any creature. No creature can ever possess an incommunicable attribute of almighty God.

Aseity

The ultimate difference between God and other beings lies in the fact that creatures are derived, contingent, and dependent. However, God is not dependent. He has the power of being in and of Himself; He does not derive it from something else. This attribute is called God's *aseity*, from the Latin *a sei*, meaning "from oneself."

Scripture tells us that in God "we live and move and have our being" (Acts 17:28), but nowhere are we told that God has His being in man. He has never needed us to survive or to be, and yet we cannot survive for an instant without the power of His being upholding our being. God created us, which means that from our first breath we are dependent upon Him for our very existence. What God creates, He also sustains and preserves, so we are as dependent upon God for our continuing existence as we were for our original existence. This is the supreme difference between God and us; God has no such dependence upon anything outside of Himself.

In an essay, the philosopher John Stuart Mill rebutted the classical cosmological argument for the existence of God, which holds that every effect must have a cause, the ultimate cause being God Himself. Mill said that if every-thing has to have a cause, then God had to have a cause, so to carry the argument all the way through, we cannot stop with God but have to ask who caused God. Bertrand Russell was convinced by the cosmological argument until he read Mill's essay. The argument Mill put forth was an epiphany for Russell, and he used it in his book *Why I Am Not a Christian*.

Mill was wrong, however. His insight was based on a false understanding of the law of causality. This law affirms that every effect must have a cause, not that everything that is must have a cause. The only thing that requires a cause is an effect, and an effect requires a cause by defini-tion because that is what an effect is—something caused by something else. But does God require a cause? He does not, because He has His being in and of Himself; He is eternal and self-existent.

The aseity of God is what defines the supremacy of the Supreme Being. Human beings are fragile. If we go a few days without water or a few minutes without oxygen, we die. Likewise, human life is susceptible to all kinds of diseases that can destroy it. But God cannot die. God is not dependent on anything for His being. He has the very power of being in and of Himself, which is what human beings lack. We wish we had the power to keep ourselves alive forever, but we do not. We are dependent beings. God and God alone has aseity.

Reason compellingly demands a being who possesses aseity; without it, nothing could exist in this world. There never could have been a time when nothing existed, because if there ever was such a time, nothing could exist now. Those who teach that the universe came into being fourteen billion years ago think in terms of self-creation, which is irrational, because nothing can create itself. The fact that there is something now means that there has always been a being.

A blade of grass screams of the aseity of God. The aseity is not in the grass itself. Aseity is an incommunicable attribute. God cannot impart His eternality to a creature, because anything that has a beginning in time is, by definition, not eternal. We can be given eternal life going forward, but we cannot get it retroactively. We are not eternal creatures.

Eternality, as such, is an incommunicable attribute. God's immutability is linked with His aseity because God is eternally what He is and who He is. His being is incapable of mutation or change. We, as creatures, are mutable and finite. God could not create another infinite being because there can be only one infinite being.

Worthy of Praise

God's incommunicable attributes point to the way in which God is different from us and the way in which He transcends us. His incommunicable attributes reveal why we owe Him glory, honor, and praise. We stand up and give accolades to people who excel for a moment and then are heard no more, and yet the One who has the very power of being in and of Himself eternally, upon whom every one of us is absolutely dependent and to whom we owe our everlasting gratitude for every breath of air that we take, does not receive the honor and glory from His creatures that He so richly deserves. The One who is supreme deserves the obedience and the worship of those whom He has made.

Chapter Five

Communicable Attributes

God's incommunicable attributes, those not shared by creatures, include His infinity, eternality, omnipresence, and omniscience. There are other attributes, however, that can be reflected in created beings, as the Apostle Paul makes clear: "Therefore be imitators of God, as beloved children. And walk in love, as Christ loved us and gave himself up for us, a fragrant offering and sacrifice to God" (Eph. 5:1–2).

Paul calls the believer to imitate God. We can imitate

God only if there are certain things about God that we have the ability to reflect. This text in Ephesians assumes that God possesses certain attributes that are communicable; that is, attributes that we have the ability to possess and manifest.

Holiness

The Scriptures say that God is holy. The term *holy*, as it is used in the Bible to describe God, refers to both His nature and His character. Primarily, God's holiness refers to His greatness and His transcendence, to the fact that He is above and beyond anything in the universe. In that regard, the holiness of God is incommunicable. He alone in His being transcends all created things. Secondarily, the word *holy*, as it is applied to God, refers to His purity, His absolute moral and ethical excellence. This is what God has in mind when He commands holiness from His creatures: "Be holy, for I am holy" (Lev. 11:44; 1 Peter 1:16).

When we are grafted into Christ, we are renewed inwardly by the Holy Spirit. The third person of the Trinity is called "holy" in part because His primary task in the Trinitarian work of redemption is to apply the work of

Christ to us. He is the One who regenerates us and the One who works for our sanctification. The Holy Spirit works in us and through us to bring us into conformity with the image of Christ, that we might fulfill the mandate for holiness that God has imposed upon us.

In our fallen state, we are anything but holy; nevertheless, through the ministry of the Holy Spirit, we are being made holy, and we look toward our glorification, when we will be completely sanctified, purified of all sin. In that sense, we are imitators of God. Even in our glorified state, however, we will still be creatures; we will not be divine beings.

Love

When Paul speaks of our responsibility to be imitators of God, he mentions that we are called to manifest love (Eph. 5:2). The Scriptures tell us that God is love (1 John 4:8, 16). The love of God is descriptive of His character; it is one of His moral attributes, and therefore it is a quality that does not belong to God alone but is communicated to His creatures. God is love, and love is of God, and all who love in the sense of the *agapē* of which the Scriptures speak are born of God. His love is an attribute that can be imitated, and we are called to do just that.

Goodness

The goodness of God is another moral attribute that we are called to emulate, though the Scriptures give a grim description of our ability in this regard. A rich young ruler asked Jesus, "Good Teacher, what must I do to inherit eternal life?" Jesus responded, "Why do you call me good? No one is good except God alone" (Mark 10:17–18). Jesus was not denying His deity here, but simply asserting the ultimate goodness of God. Elsewhere, the Apostle Paul, quoting the psalmist, says, "None is righteous, no, not one" (Rom. 3:10). In our fallen condition, we do not imitate or reflect this aspect of God's character. Yet believers are called to a life of good works, so with the help of the Holy Spirit, we can grow in goodness and reflect this aspect of God's nature.

Justice and Righteousness

There are other communicable attributes of God that we are to imitate. One is justice. When justice is spoken of in biblical categories, it is never as an abstract concept that exists above and beyond God, and to which God Himself is bound to conform. Rather, in the Scriptures, the concept of justice is linked with the idea of righteousness, and it is based on the internal character of God. The fact that God is just means that He always acts according to righteousness.

Theologians make a distinction between the internal righteousness or justice of God and the external righteousness or justice of God. When God acts, He always does what is right. In other words, He always does that which is in conformity with justness. In the Bible, justice is distinguished from mercy and grace. I used to tell my students never to ask God for justice, because they might get it. If we were to be treated by God according to His justice, we would all perish. That is why, when we stand before God, we plead that He would treat us according to His mercy and grace.

Justice defines God's righteousness; He never punishes people more severely than the crimes they have committed deserve, and He never fails to reward those to whom a reward is due. He always operates justly; never does God do anything that is unjust.

There are two universal categories: justice and non-justice. Everything outside the circle of justice is in the category of nonjustice, but there are different kinds of nonjustice. The mercy of God is outside the circle of justice and is a kind of nonjustice. Also in this category is injustice. Injustice is evil; an act of injustice violates the principles of righteousness. If God were to do something unfair, He would be acting unjustly. Abraham knew the impossibility of that when he said to God, "Shall not the Judge of all the earth do what is just?" (Gen. 18:25). Because God is a just judge, all His judgments are according to righteousness, so that He never acts in an unjust way; He never commits an injustice.

People get confused, however, when considering this alongside of God's mercy and grace, because grace is not justice. Grace and mercy are outside the category of justice, but they are not inside the category of injustice. There is nothing wrong with God's being merciful; there is nothing evil in His being gracious. In fact, in one sense, we have to extend this. Even though justice and mercy are not the same thing, justice is linked to righteousness, and righteousness may at times include mercy and grace. The reason we need to distinguish between them is that justice is necessary to righteousness, but mercy and grace are actions God takes freely. God is never required to be merciful or gracious. The moment we think that God owes us grace or mercy, we are no longer thinking about grace or mercy. Our minds tend to trip there so that we confuse mercy and grace with justice. Justice may be owed, but mercy and grace are always voluntary.

In terms of God's external righteousness or justice and His internal righteousness or justice, God always does what is right. His actions, His external behavior, always correspond to His internal character. Jesus put it simply when He told His disciples that a corrupt tree cannot produce good fruit; corrupt fruit comes from a corrupt tree, and good fruit comes from a good tree (Matt. 7:17–18). Just so, God always acts according to His character, and His character is altogether righteous. Therefore, everything He does is righteous. There is a distinction between His internal righteousness and His external righteousness, between who He is and what He does, though they are connected.

The same is true of us. We are not sinners because we sin; we sin because we are sinners. There is something flawed about our inner character. When the Holy Spirit changes us inwardly, that change is evidenced in an outward change of behavior. We are called to conform outwardly to the righteousness of God because we have been made as creatures in the image of God, with the capacity for righteousness. We have been made with the capacity to do what is right and to act in a just fashion. The prophet Micah wrote, "What does the Lord require of you but to do justice, and to love kindness, and to walk humbly with your God?" (Mic. 6:8). God's justice and righteousness are communicable attributes that we are called to emulate.

Wisdom

I want to make reference to one more of God's communicable attributes—wisdom. God is seen as not only wise but as all-wise, and we are told to act according to wisdom. The body of Old Testament literature that falls between the Historical Books and the Prophets is called the Wisdom Literature, and it includes Job, Psalms, Proverbs, Ecclesiastes, and Song of Solomon.

Proverbs tells us that the fear of the Lord is the beginning of wisdom (Prov. 9:10). For the Jew, the very essence of biblical wisdom was found in godly living, not in clever knowledge. In fact, the Old Testament makes a distinction between knowledge and wisdom. We are told to get knowledge, but above all we are told to get wisdom. The purpose of gaining knowledge is to become wise in the sense of knowing how to live in a way that is pleasing to God. God Himself never makes foolish decisions or behaves in a foolish manner. There is no foolishness in His character or activity. We, on the other hand, are filled with foolishness. Yet wisdom is a communicable attribute, and God Himself is the fountainhead and source of all wisdom. If we lack wisdom, we are called to pray that God, in His wisdom, would illuminate our thinking (James 1:5). He gives us His Word that we might be wise.

Chapter Six

The Will
of God

Several years ago, Ligonier Ministries hosted a short question-and-answer radio program called "Ask R.C.," and the question I was asked more than any other was, "How can I know the will of God for my life?" Those who are earnest in their Christian faith and want to live in obedience to Him desire to know what God wants them to do.

Whenever we find ourselves struggling over the will of God for our lives, we do well to begin with these words from Scripture: "The secret things belong to the Lord our

God, but the things that are revealed belong to us and to our children forever, that we may do all the words of this law" (Deut. 29:29). The location of that verse in Scripture is important. The book of Deuteronomy is the second book of the law; its title means "second law." It contains a recapitulation of the entire law that Moses delivered from God to the people. Near the conclusion of this account of the giving of the law, we find this text that makes a distinction between the hidden will of God and the revealed will of God.

Things Secret and Things Revealed

The Reformers, Martin Luther in particular, talked about the difference between the *Deus absconditus* and the *Deus revelatus*. There are limits to our knowledge of God; as we have seen, we do not have a comprehensive knowledge of Him. God has not revealed to us everything that could possibly be known about Him or about His intentions for the world; much of that is unrevealed. This hiddenness of God is called the *Deus absconditus*, that which God has concealed from us. At the same time, we are not left totally in the dark to grope after an understanding of God. It is not as if God has run away and failed to disclose anything about Himself. On the contrary, there is also what Luther referred to as the *Deus revelatus*, that part of God that He has revealed. That principle is revealed in Deuteronomy 29:29. "The secret things" refers to what we call "the hidden will" of God.

One aspect of the will of God is His decretive will, which refers to the fact that God sovereignly brings to pass whatsoever He wills. Sometimes this is called the absolute will of God, the sovereign will of God, or the efficacious will of God. When God decrees sovereignly that something should come to pass, it must indeed come to pass. Another way to speak of this is the "determinate forecounsel" of God. One example of this is the crucifixion. When God decreed that Christ should die on the cross in Jerusalem at a particular time in history, it had to come to pass at that place and time. It came to pass through the determinate counsel or will of God. It was irresistible; it had to happen. Likewise, when God called the world into existence, it came into existence.

There is also the preceptive will of God. Whereas the decretive will of God cannot be resisted, we not only can resist the preceptive will of God but we do resist it all the time. The preceptive will of God refers to God's law, to His commandments. The first commandment, "You shall have no other gods before me" (Ex. 20:3), for example, is part of the preceptive will of God.

When people ask me how they can know the will of God for their lives, I ask them which will they are talking about—the hidden, decretive will of God or the preceptive will of God. If they are talking about the hidden will of God, they must understand that it is hidden. Most of those who ask the question are struggling with what to do in particular situations. When I am asked about God's will in such cases, I reply that I cannot read God's mind. However, I can read God's Word, which gives me His revealed will, and learning and conforming to that will is enough of a task to last me a lifetime. I can help people with that, but not with knowing His hidden will. John Calvin said that when God "closes his holy mouth, let us also stop the way, that we may not go farther." Translating that into modern nomenclature, we would say, "The hidden will of God is none of our business." That is why it is hidden.

It is indeed a virtue to desire to know what God wants you to do. He has a secret plan for your life that is absolutely none of your business, but He may lead you and direct your paths. So there is nothing wrong with seeking the illumination of the Holy Spirit, or the leading of God, in our lives, and that is usually what people are concerned with when they ask about God's will. However, we tend to have an ungodly desire to know the future. We want to know the end from the beginning, which is indeed none of our business. It is God's business, which is why He is so severe in His warnings in Scripture against those who try to find out the future through illicit means such as Ouija boards, fortune-tellers, and tarot cards. Those things are off-limits for Christians.

Living God's Will

What does the Bible say about God's leading? It says that if we acknowledge God in all our ways, He will direct our paths (Prov. 3:5–6). We are encouraged by Scripture to learn the will of God for our lives, and we do so by focusing our attention not on the decretive will of God but on the preceptive will of God. If you want to know God's will for your life, the Bible tells you: "This is the will of God, your sanctification" (1 Thess. 4:3). So when people wonder whether to take a job in Cleveland or in San Francisco, or whether to marry Jane or Martha, they should study closely the preceptive will of God. They should study the law of God to learn the principles by which they are to live their lives from day to day.

The psalmist writes, "Blessed is the man who walks not in the counsel of the wicked, nor stands in the way of sinners, nor sits in the seat of scoffers; but his delight is in the law of the Lord, and on his law he meditates day and night" (Ps. 1:1–2). The godly man's delight is in the preceptive will of God, and one so focused will be like "a tree planted by streams of water that yields its fruit in its season" (v. 3). The ungodly, however, are not like that but "are like chaff that the wind drives away" (v. 4).

If you want to know which job to take, you have to master the principles. As you do, you will discover that it is God's will that you make a sober analysis of your gifts and talents. Then you are to consider whether a particular job is in keeping with your gifts; if it is not, you should not accept it. In that case, the will of God is that you look for a different job. The will of God is also that you match your vocation—your calling—with a job opportunity, and that requires a lot more work than using a Ouija board. It means applying the law of God to all the various things in life.

When it comes to deciding whom to marry, you look at everything Scripture says with respect to God's blessing on marriage. Having done that, you might discover that there are several prospects who meet the biblical requirements. So which one do you marry? The answer to that is easy: whichever one you want to marry. As long as the one you choose falls within the parameters of the preceptive will of God, you have complete liberty to act according to whatever pleases you, and you do not need to lose any sleep wondering whether you are outside the hidden or decretive will of God. First, you cannot be outside the decretive will of God. Second, the only way you are going to know the hidden will of God for you today is to wait until tomorrow, and tomorrow will make it clear to you because you can look back on the past and know that whatever happened in the past is the outworking of the hidden will of God. In other words, we only know God's hidden will after the fact. We usually want to know the will of God in terms of the future, whereas the emphasis in Scripture is on the will of God for us in the present, and that has to do with His commands.

"The secret things" belong to God, not to us. "The secret things" are not our business because they are not our property; they are His. However, God has taken some of the secret plans of His mind and removed the secrecy, and such things do belong to us. He has taken the veil away. This is what we call revelation. A revelation is a disclosure of that which once was hidden.

The knowledge that is ours through revelation properly belongs to God, but God has given it to us. That is what Moses was saying in Deuteronomy 29:29. The secret things belong to God, but that which He has revealed belongs to us, and not only to us but to our children. God has been pleased to reveal certain things to us, and we have the unspeakable blessing of sharing those things with our children and others. The priority of passing that knowledge on to our children is one of the main emphases in Deuteronomy. God's revealed will is given in and through His preceptive will, and this revelation is given that we might be obedient.

As I said earlier, many people ask me how they can know the will of God for their lives, but rarely does anyone ask me how he can know the law of God. People do not ask because they know how to understand the law of God— they find it in the Bible. They can study the law of God in order to know it. The more difficult question is how we can keep the law of God. Some are concerned about that, but not too many. Most people who inquire about the will of God are seeking knowledge of the future, which is closed. If you want to know the will of God in terms of what God authorizes, what God is pleased with, and what God will bless you for, again, the answer is found in His preceptive will, the law, which is clear.

One of the chief values of the Old Testament law for the New Testament Christian is that it reveals the character of God and what is pleasing to Him. We can study the Old Testament law when we are trying to find out what pleases God, and even though some of that legislation is not repeated in the New Testament, the unveiling of the character of God is there, and in it we have a lamp for our feet and a light for our path (Ps. 119:105). If we are looking for our way and groping in darkness as we seek to know the will of God for our lives, we need a lamp to show us where to go, a light to show us the pathway for our feet. It is found in the preceptive will of God. The will of God is that we obey every word that proceeds from His mouth.

Chapter Seven

Providence

Most Christians are familiar with Paul's words in Romans: "We know that for those who love God all things work together for good, for those who are called according to his purpose" (8:28). What jumps out is the strength of conviction the Apostle expresses here. He does not say, "I sure hope that everything will come out well in the end," or, "I believe things will work out according to the will of God." Instead, he says, "We know that for those who love God all things work together for good, for those who are called according to his purpose." He writes with such an Apostolic assurance about something so basic to the Christian life that we can derive great comfort from this verse.

However, I fear that today, the strength of conviction Paul expresses is very much absent from our churches and Christian communities. There has been a striking change in our understanding of the way in which our lives relate to the sovereign government of God.

I once watched a television miniseries about the Civil War. One of the most moving segments of that series occurred when the narrator read letters sent from soldiers on both sides of that conflict. As these soldiers wrote home to their loved ones, they mentioned their concerns and their fears, yet they made frequent mention of their trust in a good and benevolent God. When people settled this country, they named a Rhode Island city "Providence." That would not happen in our culture today. The idea of divine providence has all but disappeared from our culture, which is tragic.

God for Us

One way in which the secular mind-set has made inroads into the Christian community is through the worldview that assumes that everything happens according to fixed natural causes, and God, if He is actually there, is above and beyond it all. He is just a spectator in heaven looking down, perhaps cheering us on but exercising no immediate control over what happens on earth. Historically, however, Christians have had an acute sense that this is our Father's world and that the affairs of men and nations, in the final analysis, are in His hands. That is what Paul is expressing in Romans 8:28—a sure knowledge of divine providence. "And we know that for those who love God all things work together for good, for those who are called according to his purpose."

Immediately thereafter, Paul moves into a predestination sequence: "For those whom he foreknew he also predestined to be conformed to the image of his Son, in order that he might be the firstborn among many brothers. And those whom he predestined he also called, and those whom he called he also justified, and those whom he justified he also glorified" (vv. 29–30). Then Paul concludes: "What then shall we say to these things?" (v. 31a). In other words, what should be our response to the sovereignty of God and to the fact that He is working out a divine purpose in this world and in our lives? The world repudiates that truth, but Paul answers this way:

If God is for us, who can be against us? He who did not spare his own Son but gave him up for us all, how will he not also with him graciously give us all things? Who shall bring any charge against God's elect? It is God who justifies. Who is to condemn? Christ Jesus is the one who died—more than that, who was raised—who is at the right hand of God, who indeed is interceding for us. Who shall separate us from the love of Christ? Shall tribulation, or distress, or persecution, or famine, or nakedness, or danger, or sword? . . . No, in all these things we are more than conquerors through him who loved us. (vv. 31b–37)

One of the oldest sayings of the ancient church summarizes the essence of the relationship between God and His people: *Deus pro nobis.* It means "God for us." That is what the doctrine of providence is all about. It is God's being for His people. "What then shall we say to these things?" Paul asks. If God is for us, who can be against us, and who can separate us from the love of Christ? Is it going to be distress, peril, the sword, persecution, suffering, sickness, or human hostility? Paul is saying that no matter what we have to endure in this world as Christians, nothing has the power to sever the relationship we have to a loving and sovereign providence.

The word *providence* is made up of a prefix and a root. The root comes from the Latin *videre*, from which we get the English word *video*. Julius Caesar famously said, "*Veni, vidi, vici*"—"I came, I saw, I conquered." The *vidi* in that statement, "I saw," comes from *videre*, which means "to see." That is why we call television "video." The Latin word *provideo*, from which we get our word *providence*, means "to see beforehand, a prior seeing, a foresight." However, theologians make a distinction between the foreknowledge of God and the providence of God. Even though the word *providence* means the same thing etymologically as the word *foreknowledge*, the concept covers significantly more ground than the idea of foreknowledge. In fact, the closest thing to this Latin word in our language is the word *provision*.

Consider what the Bible says about the responsibility of the head of a family: "If anyone does not provide for his relatives, and especially for members of his household, he has denied the faith and is worse than an unbeliever" (1 Tim. 5:8). The responsibility is given to the head of the household to be the one who provides and makes provision; that is, that person has to know in advance what the family is going to need in terms of the essentials of life, then meet those needs. When Jesus said, "Do not be anxious about your life, what you will eat or what you will drink, nor about your body, what you will put on" (Matt. 6:25), He was not advocating a careless approach to life. He was talking about anxiety. We are not to be frightened; we are to put our trust in the God who will meet our needs. At the same time, God entrusts a responsibility to heads of households to be provident, that is, to consider tomorrow and to make sure there is food and clothing for the family.

The first time we find the word *providence* in the Old Testament is in the narrative of Abraham's offering of Isaac upon the altar. God called Abraham to take his son Isaac, whom he loved, to a mountain and offer him as a sacrifice. Quite naturally, Abraham anguished under a great internal struggle with God's command, and as Abraham prepared to obey, Isaac asked him, "Behold, the fire and the wood, but where is the lamb for a burnt offering?" (Gen. 22:7). Abraham replied, "God will provide for himself the lamb for a burnt offering, my son" (v. 8). Abraham spoke here of *Jehovah jireh*, "God will provide." That is the first time the Bible speaks of God's providence, which has to do with God's making a provision for our needs. And of course, this passage looks forward to the ultimate provision He has made by virtue of His divine sovereignty, the supreme Lamb who was sacrificed on our behalf.

Providence and Aseity

The doctrine of providence covers several areas. First, it covers the sustenance of creation. When we read the creation narrative in Genesis, that God created all things, the Hebrew word translated "create," *bara*, means more than God's simply making things and stepping out of the picture. It means that what God creates and brings into being, He then sustains and preserves. Therefore, not only are we dependent on God for our origin, but we also are dependent on God for our moment-by-moment existence.

We noted in an earlier chapter that the chief incommunicable attribute of God is His aseity, His self-existence. God alone has the power of being within Himself. Systematic theology comes into play when we consider God's aseity alongside His power of creation. The fact that God sustains what He makes reveals the relationship between the doctrine of providence and the doctrine of aseity. In Him we live and move and have our being (Acts 17:28). We are dependent upon God, who sustains and preserves us.

Our culture has been heavily influenced by the pagan view that nature operates according to fixed independent laws, as if the universe were an impersonal machine that somehow came together through chance. There is the law of gravity, the laws of thermodynamics, and other powers that keep everything operating; there is an infrastructure to the universe that makes it continue. However, the biblical view is that there could not be a universe in the first place apart from the divine act of creation, and when God created the universe, He did not step out of the picture and let it operate on its own. What we call "the laws of nature" merely reflect the normal way in which God sustains or governs the natural world. Perhaps the most wicked concept that has captured the minds of modern people is the belief that the universe operates by chance. That is the nadir of foolishness.

Chance is simply a word that describes mathematical possibilities. Chance is not a thing. It has no power. It cannot do anything, and therefore it cannot influence anything, yet some have taken the word *chance*, which has no power, and used it as a replacement for the concept of God. But the truth, as the Bible makes clear, is that nothing happens by chance and that all things are under the sovereign government of God, which is exceedingly comforting to the Christian who understands it.

I worry about tomorrow, and that is a sin. I worry about my health, and that, too, is a sin. We are not supposed to worry, but it is natural to worry about painful things and about the loss of things we value. We do not want to lose our loved ones, our health, our safety, or our possessions, but even if we do, God is working all things for our good. Even our sicknesses and losses in this world come under the providence of God, and it is a good providence.

We find that hard to believe because we are shortsighted. We feel the pain and loss now, and we do not see the end from the beginning, as God does, yet God tells us that the sufferings we have to endure in this world are not worthy to be compared with the glory He has laid up for His people in heaven (Rom. 8:18). Knowledge of divine providence brings comfort in our suffering. God is in control not only of the universe and its operations but also of history. The Bible tells us that God raises up kingdoms and brings them down, and our individual station in life has to do, in the final analysis, with what God in His providence has ordained for us. Our lives are in His hands, our vocations are in His hands, as are our prosperity or our poverty—He governs all these things in His wisdom and goodness.

Concurrence

Perhaps the most difficult aspect of providence is the doctrine of concurrence, which, in one sense, is the fact that everything that happens, even our sin, is the will of God. As soon as we say that, we could be guilty of making God the author of evil and blaming Him for our wickedness. God is not the author of sin, yet even my sin is worked out under the sovereign authority of God.

We see a clear example of this doctrine in the story of the patriarch Joseph in Genesis. As a young man, he was radically violated by his jealous brothers, who sold him to a caravan of traders making their way down to Egypt. Joseph was purchased at the slave market and then falsely accused of attacking his master's wife, which landed him in prison for many years. He was eventually released, however, and because of his great abilities and by the hand of God upon him, he was elevated to the level of prime minister over all of Egypt.

Then came a great famine. Back in Canaan, Joseph's brothers, the sons of Jacob, were starving, so Jacob sent his sons to Egypt to try to purchase food. The brothers encountered Joseph, but Joseph concealed his identity from them for a period. Eventually the truth came out, and the brothers realized that the prime minister of Egypt from whom they needed aid was the brother they had wronged years ago. They were terrified that Joseph would enact vengeance upon them, but Joseph did not. Instead he said:

I am your brother, Joseph, whom you sold into Egypt. And now do not be distressed or angry with yourselves because you sold me here, for God sent me before you to preserve life. For the famine has been in the land these two years, and there are yet five years in which there will be neither plowing nor harvest. And God sent me before you to preserve for you a remnant on earth, and to keep alive for you many survivors. So it was not you who sent me here, but God. He has made me a father to Pharaoh, and lord of all his house and ruler over all the land of Egypt. (Gen. 45:4–8)

Later, after the death of Jacob, Joseph reassured his brothers again, once more stressing the divine intent behind their evil actions:

Do not fear, for am I in the place of God? As for you, you meant evil against me, but God meant it for good, to bring it about that many people should be kept alive, as they are today. (50:19–20)

That is the great mystery of providence—a concurrence. In the mystery of divine providence, God works His will even through our intentional decisions. When Joseph said, "You meant evil against me, but God meant it for good," he meant that although his brothers had intended something evil, the good providence of God stood above that, and God was working through their wickedness for the good of the people. We see the same thing in the New Testament with Judas. Judas betrayed Jesus for evil, but God was using the sin of Judas to bring about our salvation.

That is the great comfort of the doctrine of providence, that God stands over all things and works them together for the good of His people (Rom. 8:28), and He is the ultimate source of our comfort.

About the Author

Dr. R.C. Sproul was founder of Ligonier Ministries, founding pastor of Saint Andrew's Chapel in Sanford, Fla., first president of Reformation Bible College, and executive editor of *Tabletalk* magazine. His radio program, *Renewing Your Mind*, is still broadcast daily on hundreds of radio stations around the world and can also be heard online. He was author of more than one hundred books, including *The Holiness of God, Chosen by God,* and *Everyone's a Theologian*. He was recognized throughout the world for his articulate defense of the inerrancy of Scripture and the need for God's people to stand with conviction upon His Word.

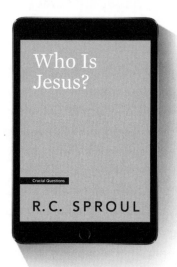